The House on Breakaheart Road

Western Literature Series

Also by Gailmarie Pahmeier

With Respect for Distance (chapbook)

The House on Breakaheart Road (limited edition)

The House on
Breakaheart Road

POEMS BY *Gailmarie Pahmeier*

▲▲ University of Nevada Press / Reno & Las Vegas

Western Literature Series

University of Nevada Press, Reno, Nevada 89557 USA
Copyright © 1981, 1987, 1988, 1989, 1990, 1991, 1992,
1993, 1995, 1996, 1997, 1998 by Gailmarie Pahmeier
All rights reserved
Manufactured in the United States of America
Design by Carrie Nelson House

Library of Congress Cataloging-in-Publication Data
Pahmeier, Gailmarie, 1957–
    The house on Breakaheart Road : poems / by
Gailmarie Pahmeier.
        p. cm. — (Western literature series)
        ISBN 0-87417-313-2 (alk. paper)
        1. Women—United States—Poetry. I. Title.
II. Series.
        PS3566.A3385H68   1998   97-32319
        811'.54—dc21   CIP

The paper used in this book meets the requirements
of American National Standard for Information
Sciences—Permanence of Paper for Printed Library
Materials, ANSI Z39.48–1984. Binding materials were
selected for strength and durability.

First Printing
07 06 05 04 03 02 01 00 99 98   5 4 3 2 1

for my sisters

our lives will never shine

with the wonderful light of inevitability.

That's all right.

—Hunt Hawkins

Contents

Acknowledgments

The author thanks the publishers of the periodicals and anthologies in which some of these poems first appeared, some in earlier versions: "The Swing," *Tar River Poetry* (Spring 1981); "In a Small Tavern Off Highway 395, Emma Gives This Guy Her Best Ear," *Interim* (Spring/Summer 1996); "When You Love Someone for a Long Time," *Northern Contours* (Spring 1997); "Take This Advice" and "Photograph of Her Parents, Dancing: 1956," *Slipstream* (1996); "Coming Home from Niagara Falls," "For an Anniversary," and "Grief Comes in the Smallest Ways," *neon* (1993–94); "Lines Too Long for a Postcard," "Her Kiss, Redeemed," and "Emma Remembers Something of the World Series," *The North Stone Review* (1993); "Kind of Like Camping: A Love Story," *Sun Dog: The Southeast Review* (1992); "Having Gone Alone to Her Hotel Room After the Conference, An Aging Professor Suffers Through Her Prayers," *If I Had My Life to Live Over* (Watsonville, Calif.: Papier-Mache Press, 1992); "With Respect for Distance," *Desert Wood: An Anthology of Nevada Poets* (Reno: University of Nevada Press, 1991); "Sunday Baking" and "Neighbors," *Seven Nevada Poets* (Reno: Black Rock Press, 1990); "Telephone Call," *Minneapolis Review of Baseball* (1990); "Sometimes Our Gifts Are Small and Fast," *Snake Nation Review* (Fall 1990); "Remember This," *neon* (Summer 1989); "Bow Fishing with My Sister" and "The Wife of Noah Comforts the Young Bride of Their Son," *Karamu* (Spring 1989); "Out Walking," *The Redneck Review of Literature* (Fall 1988); "Recalling Warm Weather," *Southwestern American Literature* (Spring 1987); "Miracle of Earth," "And I Like the Sucking Sound the Air Brakes Make," "For My Sister,

Brenda: To Be Read While Riding in the Pickup to North Carolina," and "This, The Body," *Interim* (Spring 1987).

The author would also like to thank the Nevada State Council on the Arts for financial support during the time many of these poems were written; the Mary Anderson Center for the Arts for valuable studio time; Robert Merrill and Vonnie Rosendahl for professional support; and Larry Henry for his enduring patience.

For Men

Without Sons

There Is

Always This

PART I

Photograph of Her Parents, Dancing: 1956

A blond woman in the peopled background
is smiling, her curls hugging her face
like ivy. My father holds my mother
against his chest, a calm and grateful
twist to his lips. His hand is knuckled
around hers, the lace wedding dress
burning upon his shirt. My mother's eyes
are open large, her lips drawn thin.
Her light-filled face contrasts his shadowed dark,
as if she is aware that in a mere
few hours, she will be a mother in the most
elemental way, that three months later
she will pull this man from a pool hall, say
I thought you knew.

What she doesn't know is that over thirty
years later she will still find some ways
to love him, that she will happen upon
the occasional day when she can say
out loud, *I like this, living with him.*
What she doesn't know is that the child
will be an only, silent and tearful,
that the house will ache with this child's angry
fear and desperately lovely dreaming.
What she doesn't know is that a day
is coming when she will sit in the thick
Kentucky air placing bets on horses
she chooses for name, she chooses for me, for her

distant daughter, for all the hope and luck
and fury she owned in the blurred still
of the photograph. She chooses *Wild Girl,
Angel of Energy*, she chooses *Eager Love*.

She doesn't know, she has no idea
that I will turn out this bad, so like her
in her darker, picture-perfect heart.

Fathers with Daughters

Watching this one now in her painless sleep,
you imagine your eyes, her mother's limbs,
an odd mesh of familiarity.
A director with only an actor,
no script, you've a definite job to do.
Be precise, be consistent. Hold her head
in your lap in the late afternoon,
tell her she's lovely as soon as you're sure
she understands somehow what that might mean.
Your daughters are a perilous treasure,
an uncertain pleasure, a certain wish,
a work to be criminally proud of.
For men without sons there is always this.

Barbie, Ken, and Emma's Daddy

Other girls have friends to share their dolls.
Here in the closed air of an afternoon
at the lake, Emma has her daddy,
sun-browned and deliciously worn
from the early hours of setting trotline.
He drinks beer after beer to cool him, dabs
at the fat drops of sweat along his neck,
his chest, his brow. Other girls have mommas
to sing them songs, to wash the dried day off
their unedited skin. Emma's momma's gone,
three weeks already into Idaho,
and Emma, who has waited near lifetimes
for toys ordered off the backs of cereal
boxes, knows that eight weeks is eternity.
But it's okay. Barbie's here and Ken's come
along. They've been to the store and gone
skating and gotten lost in the deep woods,
Ken built Barbie a house, they have children
made of sticks, two rock dogs and an acorn cat.
Later they will take their wickedly smooth
bodies to bed where Ken will snore and Barbie
will turn from side to side, choose moonlight,
not sleep, drink coffee, smoke cigarettes.
But first there will be dancing. After supper
Emma's daddy plays the radio,
takes Ken in his big hands. Emma leans Barbie
near and nearer and they rock and roll
their way to weary. Every night.

This is all Emma knows now and close
enough to what she needs. There's comfort
in this honest life: sunshine, water,
a place to play, a little music,
her daddy's heavy footsteps on the dark
porch, loud as loneliness and brutally
beautiful, just like Barbie, just like Ken.

Emma Remembers Something of the World Series

Game 7, October 12, 1967 / *St. Louis, 7 Boston, 2*

She remembers the schoolboys' envy,
how her father's worn hand wrapped her own,
maneuvered her through mote-filled halls
swallowed in possibility, some hope.

She remembers her legs, how she'd pluck
them off the plastic car seats, how the hot
thick air rolled against her face,
how his cigarettes left her rich and dizzy.

She remembers the dusty smell of peanuts,
how the old man selling them on the street
winked, said *lucky doll*, told her father
eats is gettin' outrageous inside.

She remembers the sweet, wet smell of men
in suits, how they stood and shook their arms,
how someone spilled, something, on her father's shoe.
Raise your han' for the soda pop man!

Emma remembers her father never said
Girl, you'll remember this all of your life,
but she remembers he leaned into her again
and again, pointed out plays, players

how he touched her and taught her the language
of baseball: Say *balk.* Say *everyday eight.*
Say *bat handle blooper.* Say *cross over pivot.*
Say *Bob Gibson.* Say *father.* Say *daughter.*

Sometimes Our Gifts Are Small and Fast

Emma learned to drive at eighteen—
sometimes schooled by country boys in denim jackets
down endless dirt roads going nowhere but away,
sometimes taught by college boys in sweaters and
   long cars—
but always by boys whose passion
far outdistanced their patience.

Learning to drive meant learning to live.
Tall plastic glass of sugared tea
held snug between her legs,
radio full of Peggy Lee, weather reports, baseball.
Seventy miles an hour and an afternoon
brought thoughts of him, their car.

Her father lies on his back, knees up,
arms extended. Emma wants to go
downtown, wants to drive to the river,
ride around, watch some lights.
She sits on his knees, takes his left hand
as steering wheel, his right as stick shift.
Her father makes the engine sound, eyes closed.
Emma drives hard, all her windows down.
When her mother calls for dinner, tires squeal.
His legs open—a telephone pole or highway divider—
and Emma crashes into her father's embrace.
She is seven and she knows this road.

Now an atlas away from that living room,
she drives and drives faster
to meet a young man whose hands are large.
He promises to hold her, keep her safe and full and free.
He doesn't know how little she needs.
Emma's already got a car, a memory, and a place to go.

My Mother's Story About the Dog

My father, one morning as always,
went to lift the aged terrier from her bed.
Her blue-filmed eyes greeted his voice
as he carried her to the kitchen, out the door.
He watched her in the twenty-two inches of damn hard
snow, made coffee, wandered again to the window.
He saw her circle the yard, turn toward him.
He thought she saw a bird, perhaps, or simply desired
to climb into the box under the porch
where she curled against herself in warmer weather.
But she quivered, she collapsed,
dragged her body some several inches through snow.

Days later my mother found my father
missing. His coat gone, she feared he'd left
toward the store, and with so many decent men
dying doing simple chores in this cold,
she called his name into the white with heart.
She found him safely bundled, breathing hard
to smooth into a slick mound the snow
above where the dog lay. He rose before her
bringing a handful of snow to her mouth.
She ate from his palm, gathered snow to feed him.
This, she says, is what comes of it, of love.

The Swing

The yellow metal seat flashes
in the casual sun.
His four daughters, all under twelve
and desperate to be pushed,
circle around him
as he waters the garden.

Swing me, Daddy!

Swing me!

You'd shoot the hose at us.
The water was hard and cold—right for August—
but here was a sudden tilt to your laughter.
The neighbor paused to watch your girls
running, bare feet springing the dandelions,
skin sparkling and dripping.

When I pass the park at night now,
I imagine a father swinging his daughter,
pushing her higher, higher.
The park echoes long trailing screams of pleasure,
as thick familiar hands propel her small body,
her skirt opening to gather the dark.

With Respect for Distance

Before I pull into the parking lot,
I see him standing there, shirt-sleeved, pipe in hand.
Since last week he hasn't changed,
perhaps he looks a little tired.
His slow smile, and I know I'm on time.

How's she runnin'?
The certain first question, his greeting.
I give the shrug, tap the hood of my car.
There is something miraculous about this machine,
how it has come to cement a father and daughter
separated by everything but this link.

We pass the day calling trucks—
Peterbilt, Kenworth, Mack.
Small words, none as striking
as the glint of chrome beneath his determined touch.
When I leave I know he is watching me,
waiting for the sound of malfunction.

What will I tell my children when he is gone?
He was a quiet man who could make things run.

When You Love

Someone

for a Long Time

PART II

Sunday Baking

—for Miller Williams

He thinks she cannot see him through the window,
smoking his cigar in the slow Sunday dusk.
That's what these evenings are for,
smoking and reading an easy magazine.
From a chair on the porch he moves to watch her,
kneading and pulling this day's bread.
He should speak, offer his assistance.
He could grease the pans and sweep the flour dust,
pull the damp hair away from her forehead
as she smiles and stretches this thing she knows.
But the kitchen seems crowded when she works,
full of the several people she has been.
The girl whose cupped hands splashed his back,
the one whose fingers learned his skin,
the woman whose whole body is in this baking.
It is the hands of this woman that haunt him.
Although it is a damn thing, it carries him.
The bread's in the oven, and the smell
of love is thick inside, and he knows
that the bread, the woman, and the house are not his,
that this is what is meant by home.

For an Anniversary

still willingly I rage with you —A. Wilber Stevens

Love, if I leave our life before you,
take this, my kitchen, as legacy.
Take the cayenne, the andouille,
the boudin, the hard, hard bread.
Serve fresh vegetables steamed
with vinegar, peppers to suck
from their stems, orange spice tea.
Make sure there is ice, chicory coffee.
Give everyone, including children, cloth napkins.
After dinner there should be music,
roll up the rugs and dance.

Love, if I leave our life before you,
imagine me in the arms of a boy
whose pickup truck carries his dreams.
I'll be eating apples, leaving lipstick on cans,
listening to rain-delayed games on the radio.
Love, whatever passes, I promise —
in our old age we will not want.
Here, come here. Taste this.

The Promise of Good Food

Emma sizzles through Sparks, through Fernley
and Wadsworth and on through Oreana
and Mill City. By the time she gets
to Lovelock, she knows he'll be worried,
think she's on her way to Elko

where a serial killer haunts
the highway. But she's not going that far,
not this time. See, when Emma flies, she flies
toward food. By dark she'll make Winnemucca,
the Hotel Martin where she'll share chilled
red wine, wet salad, tongue soup, porterhouse

with people she'd never have imagined
knowing—a cowboy perhaps or a retired
couple from Sault Ste. Marie. They'll laugh
a bit and tell stories, and all
the while Emma will know that he's at home

searching through her stuff. When she takes
her second helping, he will have found
the red lace panties she's never worn,
the antique tray of Mexican rings,
the photographs of her godmother's
handsome husbands: the one who died

of gunshot, the one who fell from his horse,
the one that woman left by bus
for the city. By sherbet, he'll be

hunting for her diaries, little
locked books she pretends to keep. He'll tire

by early light, sleep heavily
and love her hard when she gets home.
This is just the way it is, and Emma
pleasures in the patterns of their life,
knows he'll stay on as long as it takes,
as long as it takes him to find something.

Coming Home from Niagara Falls

—for John Clellon Holmes

This trip isn't easy. We know, of course,
it's the last. I can tell by the way
you hold the steering wheel, as if
the lazy drifting of the car is natural.

Maybe when we arrive in Illinois
I'll get out, telephone someone from one
of those emergency aid phones—please come.
I'll call my father in Granite City.
He hasn't seen me in awhile, and he worries.

There's ice on the highway around Cleveland.
I ask to stop for a sandwich
at a truckport, but you keep driving.
I'm not asking for anything anymore
except cigarettes, and I have plenty.

Outside Indianapolis it's dark.
You turn to me, ask how I'm doing.
I say I'm fine. You say
we're making good time, and that's what matters.

Out Walking

This is one of those things I require,
a walk through night after common day.
It's easy to measure step, listen to the pattern
of someone else's feet several houses behind.
I'm unafraid; the dark is always deeper
farther on, waiting to take my legs.
Sounds out here are simple—the burn
of leaf against leaf, the battering
of bugs into light.
There's safety in these streets.
Somewhere in this neighborhood,
a woman cries into her man's thickness.
He lies there silent, thinking
if he could choose, he'd go.

Miracle of Earth

His name is Nicky and hers is Charmaine.
She spends the dawn polishing his black boots
so his legs sticking out from under his car
will have some shine and he will know she cares.
Saturday they celebrated a year.
She wanted pearls but he bought her
a used Pontiac, and that's okay.
He's going to fix it fine.
She'll be pleased to pull the brown body
into the lots of Safeway and Otasco.
Once after work he hit her hard
and left a scar the shape of a heart
exactly in the center of her forehead.
That night he brought paper carnations,
four pictures of himself from a dimestore booth.
There were days she thought she'd leave,
take a train to a city, Chicago, Tulsa.
If he loved her he'd follow the red line
she'd drawn in the old atlas.
That was then and this is now
she has planted asparagus, and he loves her name.

The Business of Knives

He made her his wife some months ago and learned
that she's obsessed by sudden terrors
that drive him to hide the kitchen knives.
This is one of the ways he loves her.
Lying next to her now in this yellow light,
he watches her face, both lovely and ludicrous.
Through the haze of her cigarette
he can see how her face will fall,
how one day he will not know this woman.
He cannot recall
how his heart turned for such frail promises,
or how she knew his love was a savage, saving cowardice.

The Mouths of Women

It's Saturday and he has nothing else to do
but sit here in this diner eating eggs.
They are prepared appropriately
and the toast is smoothly buttered,
but today his focus is on the mouths of women.
Now one bites down on a piece of bacon.
Her friend with the French braid rolls her tongue
along the side of an English muffin.
Over there sits a girl eating jelly,
a purple mass riding an iced-tea spoon.
He thinks of his own woman gone to Missouri.
He imagines the man who holds her,
how her full mouth curls, twists, and circles.
Soon he'll return to his thick slice of ham,
see how the fat glistens against the plate.

Neighbors

The typist who lives above him
tells him always she loves her work.
Once over wine she told him how cool
her fingers feel cradled in the hollows
of the keys, how the busy clacking reminds
her of a toy train her brother had,
then a real train carrying passengers
to mysterious places, like Montana.
She says, sometimes the letters as they
become words are like people running
to form a line for a movie or free food.
Even the quiet buzzing between pages
soothes her, for it is the purring of cats
that might escape all fateful drownings.
He likes this woman, she's a good neighbor.
Often in the evenings he sits to write
usually a letter to his lover
asking in another way: *Shannon, come home.*
He sets the stroke for heavy, beating down
so the sound will carry to the typist.
He imagines she's just washed her hair,
hears his plea rising through the heat vents,
pillows herself on the floor.
Her hair dries slowly as she eases into sleep.

Grief Comes in Smallest Ways

For the first time in months
she's making meat loaf.
He imagines the casual manner
in which she cracks an egg,
the way it slides down the sides
of the glass bowl to marry
beef, yellow onion, bell pepper, spice.
He imagines it is abandon
that pulls her hands
into the bowl;
he imagines it is delight
that carries her as egg soaks
into meat between her fingers.
He wishes she would wear
a short full apron,
someplace to leave the stick
she rubs from her palms.
He wishes she'd always bake meatloaf.

She works out, sweats.
She shows him often
how her arms are strong,
that with her legs
she can lift a weight
he'd have died
to save her from.
She calls from the kitchen.
He finds her sitting,
legs scissored open.

Look, she says,
and brings her chest
to rest against the floor.
You're lovely, he says.
I like the way your skin looks
pulled tight against your thigh.
I like the way the kitchen light
moves brilliant through your hair.
I like the way things smell.

Telephone Call

When Emma heard him say he didn't love her,
she thought of spring,
she thought of a spring without baseball,
what it would be like if boys who lived in towns
with names like Idabel, Osceola, or Tonopah
held smooth round rocks in their hands
without knowing how such a small dream
can send a boy to a city
of lights and noise and grateful women,
or what it would be like if the girls
who loved them never knew the hard bleachers,
or the anxious taste of chewed pencils,
never kissed a boy who left the dust
from a slide on their skin,
or what it would be like if fathers never knew
how old they were because their arms
didn't weaken, their shoulders, backs never slipped,
their sons earned pride or sadness or shame
in some less simple way,
or what it would be like if mothers
didn't stand at kitchen windows and see
their boys learn that women watch,
that a good woman will ride
all the way across the state
with a game on and never
ask for music.
When Emma heard him say he didn't love her,
she thought of dresses she had never worn.

Lines Too Long for a Postcard

One way to Fort Smith,
I tell the man, alone
in the bus stop, first time in months.
Without you I come to check less luggage,
fewer things I need, or say I need
to carry home.
I've taken a sheet — the one on which
the last decent act of love closed down upon —
taken perhaps more as prize than as memory.
I'll miss listening to your holding
vowels on your tongue
the way a child cradles a fallen bird.
I'll miss the secrets shared in darkness
that slip with light like shapes near a closet.
These are the things I'll take back,
from Shreveport, from Kansas City.
These are the things you have given me.
Sometimes I think they're enough, and I'm glad.

She Writes to Her Lover,
Whose Hair Is Thick and Clean

Here in Indiana it has rained
for five days, the sort of rain you'd call
serious, rain that comes with sound,
with light. I've felt safe in this weather,
that shaky sense of presence you own
when you wake to thunder. But the one thing
that's really on my mind is hair,

how I hardly recognize myself
in the bathroom mirror. At home
in the desert my hair hangs heavy
against my back, its dark fullness smoothed,
untangled in your fingers, a fine rope
for your love hold. But not here. Here

the wet air has created curls,
ringlets some women pay a lot for.
I had forgotten about this, the way
a place can so subtly change who you are,
bring you back to what you once were.

In grade school I knew a girl named Stella
whose grandfather promised her fifty bucks
if she could sit on her hair, resist
the urge for the fashionable pixie.
We envied her good fortune: hair that grew
quickly and a family with money.

Jolene, my cousin, would come on some
Saturday evenings to pile my mother's
hair into beehive, help her with eyeliner
and wound-red lipstick. My mother wore
a black dress, always, scarves tight around
her throat. My mother was, on occasion,
the most beautiful woman in the world.

I remember my own hair, short
and unruly, how the big boys held me
down on the playground, threatened to set me
on fire. *Spider hair*, they called it, and I
believed them, lay flat in the vacant lot
long after dark, waiting on the safety
of my father's flashlight and his tired voice.

Remember the lovely blonde with the Prell
bottle and the dropped pearl? I always
wondered if she got it out, rolled it
in her hand, brought its rich, clean smell
to her face. It's funny what you forget.
Then you're alone, there's a mirror, and it rains.

In a Town Too Cold for Baseball

In Emma's bad dream she's always old,
say thirty-five or so,
a woman whose hands are often stiff.
Always in this dream she eats pizza alone
in a neon-filled room where a boy waits tables,
brings slender glasses of beer she can wrap
her fingers around, hide her impatient polish.
Always she stays too late, eats too little,
waits with the boy for a cab to come.
But tonight he walks her through the door,
offers to drive her where she'd want to go,
says *a kiss can make it better, baby,*
presses her, presses, says *let's go, let's go.*
When Emma wakes her hair is wet,
her breath puffs white above the bed.
The older man beside her stirs,
his hands tense, relax, tense, relax.
He reaches out to touch her,
says *sleep, Emma, sleep. You breathe*
like an angel. Go back to sleep.
Emma, you're safe.

Recalling Warm Weather

The Bread Lady. The Bird Lady—
two names the neighborhood kids attached
to the old woman in the grey stone home.
Year long she laced her yard with crumbs,
a place made naturally private by trees.
Spring and summer her grounds were a clear cage,
kind refuge for ravens, jays, sparrows.
Hidden behind shrubs I watched the feeding.
She called them names: *Adelia, dear Bill, John.*

My grandfather called her Miss Lonely Coot,
said the blue flicker that marred the dark
night at her house was a television:
Only folks she knows are faces in a glass box.
One evening I went with a need to know.
The flicker came from candles in sky-toned
hurricanes. Beneath this light, framed photos,
dozens of them, facts of a life past.
She sat tearing bread into bird-sized bites.
Mary, she addressed the mantel, *how lovely
you look tonight. And Bill, he's come home.*

Emily, if hope is the thing with feathers,
memory is the open beak, this seasonal hunger.

Kind of Like Camping: A Love Story

In room 203 of the Motel 6,
Emma lies in his sweet smell, satisfied
and hungry. He spreads the other cover,
the one from the bed not yet used, between
them, removes champagne and cheese, two apples
from his backpack, brings forth a knife to slice
this, their meal. He'll feed her, tell stories.
Emma will rise and meander toward
the sink, rinse the two plastic cups and fill
them with their drinks. When she returns to him,
he'll be telling her how often the light
in the Sierra can change, how she'd find
awe in the earth, the beautiful breathing
of animals, the sounds that have no sound.
He'll say he loves her, wants her in his world,
wants to sleep outside and curl around her
under the honesty of stars. Emma loves
him, so will suffer through his dreams again.
What she wants to say is simple, too so
for a man who makes his life among mountains.
She wants to say: *Listen, love, lay me back*
here against the headboard and listen. This
is like camping, kind of. We always come
here with little luggage — combs, toothpaste, food.
We come together in your old truck, hike
the two floors to our room, you leading me,
I walking softly and quickly behind,
both of us alert to another type
of snake. At the door to our room you turn,

you smile, you take me into the brilliant
clearing where we pretend no one has been
before. Sometimes the muffled voices next door
remind us other creatures share our air,
and once while you slept a postcard fluttered
to the floor from the nightstand, a butterfly.
Remember how we found shapes, as children
do with clouds, in the ceiling's water stains?
You found a spider and I a coyote.
And one time when I awoke to find you gone,
a note that said Next time you come to me,
I stumbled toward the light, found a chair
right there in the middle of the forest.
Emma wants to tell him this, tell him there
are simpler ways to learn grace, heart, place.
Instead she says: Love, this is kind of like
camping. We're free. We have some time. He laughs.
He feeds her an apple slice with the knife.

When You Love Someone for a Long Time
—for Ruth

He has planned this road trip for no reason
except he loves her and it is summer
and he needs something to do. She sits beside
him in the truck, a basket of apples
on the floorboard, a map across her lap.
He loves Nevada, loves leaving their Midwest
home for the spare embrace of desert, open
light, loves the way the land here allows
a man to feel as if he has potential.

They've driven through Currant and Warm Springs
and he has promised that when they get
to Tonopah he will buy her dinner
in the old hotel where gamblers and boxers
have left their stories and the ghost
of a jilted woman in a red dress
wanders the third floor. He tells her next time
they will travel out to Tuscarora
or down to Boundary Peak. He does love

the land, this man. He does the driving, most
of the talk. He's trying to teach her things,
bring her closer to the world outside
of kitchen and bedroom and yard. She listens,
her hand resting on his inner thigh.
If she spoke there would be things she could tell,
things a man just somehow misses when he
travels, no matter how large his heart:

Somewhere in Smith Valley there is a road
called Breakaheart, and along its washboard
rests a greying farmhouse. She has often
imagined the woman who must live there,
perhaps her name is Hannah, how her husband
may have one day taken down the gun
and driven off. Although she would be sad,
Hannah wouldn't be surprised to hear the hounds,
the good men come to tell her she's now alone.
For three days Hannah neglects to brush her hair,
but on the fourth she is up, hanging
laundry, forgiving everyone she's ever
known and looking up into the sweet, strong sun.

But he drives, hums along to the country
stations, talks, asks her if steak will be good
tonight, a fat rare one. She smiles and nods.
These road trips are worth their dust, their
unfamiliar beds, their exaggerated
hope. These are the only times she lives
in long, luxurious stretches of time,
when she lives, utterly complete, without him.

Take This

Advice

PART III

The Wife of Noah Comforts the
Young Bride of Their Son

Come to the corner where it's warm. We'll chat.
I've seen the sadness in your face,
the dreary smile of submission you give to Ham.
Come closer. I'll tell you: I know it's okay.
While I was cleaning cages I heard them talking—
there's been a test and only our men have passed.
We are here by the mere fortune of marriage—
ours are the legs that legally wrap their backs.
It is for being women we've been saved,
slated for pleasure and parenthood.
We are important; there's no need to worry.
We'll be the reason for everything after the rain.

For My Sister, Brenda: To Be Read While Riding in the Pickup to North Carolina

This is the beginning of many nights
spent packing, days spent rambling
across the country in some old car or truck.
This is the first of all those leavings.
Take it slow.
Look closely at this Ford.
Memorize the slits in the seat,
the breathing of the dog on the floor.
Look at the man beside you.
On this trip his touch carries a promise.
Later, when you love too quickly
and he has heard you moan in the dark
hundreds of times,
it will say something else.
Memorize him.
Memorize everything:
animals rotting on the road,
women hanging clothes,
children waving, not knowing who you are.
Fold these things away.
This time everything is important.
I would not lie to you unless I needed to.

Bow Fishing with My Sister

I spend Saturdays poised on the edge of rock,
bow and line and razored point ready.
I aim for large targets; I aim for gar,
useless enough so there's no regret in wounding.
This time you've come along.

When I think of you, I think of water.
Not the still hard sort a lake holds,
nor the quick rush of what we have here.
When I think of you, I think of the warm
gray bath water shared by two sisters.

Sunday night, and we are bathing.
We sit with our legs scissored together.
Perhaps that very day,
certainly one nearby, I've learned
about breasts, that I have them.

Suddenly I think of breasts, that I have them.
I spread my washcloth across my chest,
turn my back to you.
When I rise I see you, see you
clutching your own wet cloth to your heart.

Carolyn, I know that this is foolish,
that nothing is so easily understood,
but I've often thought that if I hadn't turned
you would be well.
Men would have loved you with more grace, more

promise. Books would have told you a simpler
truth, made light for where you walked,
and even country songs which relish sadness
would have given you some joy. Small things.
Watching you now as your hair relaxes

into the wind, feeling your chill as you touch
my arm for balance, I should tell this.
Instead I say, *Here, hold steady,*
aim hard, just let it sing.
It's easy to pull an arrow back.

More Moons Than One

Nearly forty, and I have come to this.
I eat sugar doughnuts to pass the time
till the bus pulls away from Peoria.
This was not the plan when I was her age,
the girl there upon whom all eyes take ease.
Even I yearn to touch her loveliness,
trace a finger along her strict skin,
down the long neck and across the shoulder.
She must be smoking underneath her flesh,
eager to shed this city for another
where a boy waits with something like promise.
I could tell her the heart is a frail liar,
its plangent grievings no more than air.
If I speak to her, I'll just say I know.
I, too, have been with boys, and loved them.

So This Is What Happened

Hansel sleeps heavily,
his dull lips pulled
back against his teeth.
His sleep-scent is strong,
and Gretel breathes his fragrance
of homemade bread and chocolate
with hesitation.
He's been a good brother,
and though he's older only by minutes
she's done everything he's asked
forever now, for years.
Today she will take him walking
far into the Shawnee Forest
where she has met a lady
with a special recipe.

Having Gone Alone to Her Hotel Room After the Conference, An Aging Professor Suffers Through Her Prayers

—for James Whitehead

Lord, forgive me my common
dreams, my daily deceptions.
Forgive that I have feigned to bless
those books that give me bread,
that I have written save few words
which shine with any soul,
that I have somehow earned a place
solid, certain, removed from blood,
hunger and heart.
Forgive that I no longer have to pray.

And Lord, forgive my love of the boys,
the one who sings the country songs
with clarity and calm,
the one who reads every book I recommend,
the boy whose memory holds these poems
in place.
Lord, if you can forgive me this, protect
them. I promise to pray again. *Ah-men.*

Amen.

And I Like the Sucking Sound the Air Brakes Make

I've got to get somewhere again.
I carry no sign because it's simpler this way.
I deny that I'm tired, that the wet dark
has left a crown of ice in my hair.
In the flat Illinois night, I wait.
A Mack pulls to the side, idles, hums.

He doesn't offer any help.
It takes a moment to climb into the cab.
My legs are short, stiff from the cold.
He notices my shiver,
passes his ham and cheese.
We're used to people like us.

I rest my fingers in my sleeves,
allow the chill to stream down my face.
He says he has a daughter
about my age, born when he
was hardly more than a boy in Shreveport.
I tell him I'm not that young, but I can laugh
and that'll keep me moving a little longer.

Farther on, he pulls off
where orange lights flash us to STOP EAT.
I watch him move through the glaring entrance
to fill his thermos, pick up cigarettes.
I'll wait in the back for fifteen minutes.
If he wants me, he'll hurry.
I am cleaner than I look.

Why People Move

Harriet lived next door to my mother
for fifteen years. We loved her home, its utter
pinkness: Princess phone, Lady Kenmore washer,
little hairbrushes in a basket above
the bath. We also loved her hair, red
and tight against her head, the kind of hair
my mother said you worked at. Her daughter,
big and truly pink, did things with boys
that made her laugh off beyond the lilacs.
My mother said, *What do you expect?*
Names are destiny, you know: Harriet,
Elmer, Charmaine. Harriet herself
was the star checker at the A&P,
pausing between punches only to touch
her hair when stuff like artichoke hearts
or zucchini came up. Mother said those
sorts of groceries made you wonder if
you were born in the wrong town, and therefore
they were dangerous. Elmer up and left
one day, headed for Florida
and another religion. Harriet
stayed on, got her pension and her pretty
pink house, and Charmaine did seem to love her.
Days before she died, Harriet asked me
to tell the stories, tell about her quick
fingers and her good hair and how her name
was one customers remembered, being
appropriate and all. Well, okay.
I'll tell: Harriet, I live in the mountains

now and my mother's gone. I live with a good
man who has an easy smile and strong hands.
I live with a man who'll also believe
much more than anyone would ever ask him to.

In a Small Tavern Off Highway 395, She Gives This Guy Her Best Ear

—for Jim, again

Often in the season of apples,
he remembers some of the ways he loved
her, how she smoked brown cigarettes
and danced, hips rolling easy as egg yolk,
her little black dress with the frayed hem,
lovely and promising in the bar's dark,
how she wore a Stetson just this side
of too big, cowboy boots as red as her
mouth, and that mouth sure brought him hope.
She'd come into town one summer and he'd known
he'd known her before he knew her. Maybe
it was the mouth, or the way she tossed
her black hair or maybe, yes maybe,
it was her hands, hands that looked like
they'd known work, hands like his, hands
that know the good sense of a full day,
know that night should be saved for rest
and pleasure. She'd stayed all summer,
allowed herself to be taken, loved
by this man old enough to have fathered
her. That power was her gift.
But come fall, this season, she'd gone,
not given to rubbing a man's back
if it weren't about to lead to something.
But what if she'd stayed on? bellyed his child?
Given him a better chance at becoming
a good memory? Oh, hell—there are other
women, and it's not like he can't get

him some. And it's always a good thing
that seasons change and the snow comes.

He could've had a daughter somewhere by now,
and what, dear God, would he do then?

Her Kiss, Redeemed

I'm the woman who was the girl you boys beat against
out of desperate fear you might not make manhood.
Someone had to care for you.
Know that I had a large love for you all.

I've seen two names on books, one on a record,
names I whispered with heaviness along the levee.
You've gone on to become men of matter,
allowing my memory to lapse until it serves a lyric.

But I'm paid in full when I imagine
your gracious wives pulling your faces
forward for a kiss or a tear or a word,
and without pause you recall

the breeze that night,
or the smell of smoke near water,
or how your cheek was smooth then,
how in my hands your dreams came true.

This, The Body

Even with your fingers upon my thigh,
I know I am an alien among these candles,
the kneeling and rising of bodies bundled for winter.

The Christ here is cut into glass—
orange, red, blue, significant purple—
colors perfecting his pain, making it brilliant,
a satisfying and lovely agony.

I kneel. The steak scent of extinguished candles
sends me home to dinner, sweet potatoes, rolls.
The table is set in white lace and candles.
A bowl of peppermints shines out of the center.

When it comes my turn to rise, I'll go forward
and take the dry wafer onto my tongue,
leave it there to release its heaviness slowly.

Look: Christ's fingers, unlike yours, are curled.

Take This Advice

When your husband dies, vary your story.
Never settle for the uninteresting
truth. You, remember, were the woman
some fortune-teller or drunken lover
said would die in white across an expanse
of grand piano—gunshot, bad drugs.
You are not one for the gentle common.

A decent man dies, his heart a fallen cake.
Tell it better. Tell his mother he died—
Just like that—
between the patio and the back door.
He had risen to check sound—a child's cry,
perhaps, or some small wounded animal.
He was a fine man, kind and generous.

Tell your girlfriends he died on his way
to the kitchen. He had held you for hours,
you had imagined pearls and petals.
He had risen for champagne, a special
bottle he kept hidden for full moon, talk.
Just like that.
He was a romantic man, and solid.

Tell his friends he died inside of you,
moaning his blood cry, making you cling, you
both far away eating berries, rubbing sticks.
Say he was often a surprising
lover, vigorous, and terrifying.

Just like that.
He was a passionate man, hungry but sure.

Tell no one he died in his sleep, gasping
for his share of air. Tell no one you were
dreaming you were floating in cool Montana
water with a boy whose hand was wide
across your back. Tell no one he was teaching
you how water enters stone. Tell no one
you heard nothing when your whole world changed.

About the Author

Gailmarie Pahmeier teaches creative writing and literature courses at the University of Nevada, Reno, where she has been honored with the Alan Bible Teaching Excellence Award and the University Distinguished Teacher Award. Her literary awards include the Chambers Memorial Award, a Witter Bynner Foundation Poetry Fellowship, and two Artists Fellowships from the Nevada State Council on the Arts. Her work has been widely published in literary journals and anthologies.